Book 1
Malware
By Solis Tech

&

Book 2
Raspberry Pi 2
By Solis Tech

Book 1
Malware

By Solis Tech

Malware Detection & Threats Made Easy!

Malware: Malware Detection & Threats Made Easy!

Table of Contents

Introduction

I want to thank you and congratulate you for purchasing the book, *"Malware: Malware Detection & Threats Made Easy!"*.

This book contains proven steps and strategies on how to avoid, detect and remove malware.

Malware creators are very creative, employing both technical and social means to spread malware. Simply installing antivirus software is no longer enough. This book explains how malware spreads in order to arm the reader with information on how to manage its threat.

Thanks again for purchasing this book, I hope you enjoy it!

Chapter 1 – Malware

Computers are inherently dumb. They can accept and input data, can process it at high-speed, and can return the results almost instantly. However, users need to tell the computer what to do in the form of codes. We call these codes programs, applications, scripts or software, but they are essentially the same. They give instructions to the computer. What the computer does will depend on the instructions given to it. Tell it to do something useful and it will. Give it instructions to perform a malicious task and it will do it without question. Even computers with artificial intelligence are simply following instructions that simulate human's way of thinking.

Computers do not care who gives the instructions. As long as the instructions are loaded into memory, the computer will process it accordingly. Upon startup, a short set of instructions will tell the computer to load and launch the operating system or OS. The OS in turn executes startup instructions that it finds. These include preparing the input and output drivers, as well as launching other background tasks. Having done that, the OS awaits command from its user to execute other applications.

Malware developers take advantage of these key concepts. They find vulnerabilities in the operating and network system that will allow them to install malware and have it running in the background. Vulnerabilities are bugs in the program that can let malware writers load additional code and execute it. These bugs or programming errors do not always appear during the testing stage.

Some malware writers use social engineering to trick victims into installing malware into their computers. They use the computer's connection to internal and external networks to propagate the malware. They infect shared storage to spread malware among colleagues. They hack into servers to install malicious code that will infect site visitors. They can do this because computers will run any executable code that is loaded into its memory.

What is Malware?

Malware is short for malicious software. It is a general term for a code that compromises a computer and instructs it to do malicious tasks, often without the knowledge or permission from the computer's owner. Early malware refers to programming challenges and pranks like programs that delete user files, but recent malware refers to targeting servers to make them inaccessible or for financial gains.

Home computers are not safe, either. Cybercriminals are using home computers to launch attacks on servers in addition to stealing personal information to access online bank accounts. Some advertisers adopt malware, too. They no longer wait for users to visit their sites, but install malware into a victim's computer so they can modify browser settings and change the default home page, eventually advertising their products every time a user opens the browser. They sometimes change the default search engine, replacing it with engines that track user habits to benefit advertisers.

Mobile devices are not safe, either. Today's mobile devices are computers with features and capabilities that are comparable to older computers. Mobile devices, like smartphones and tablets, are vulnerable because they require applications to work. If users inadvertently download a compromised application, then there is a possibility that malware can compromise their mobile devices, too.

A future malware playground is Internet of Things. It is a term for consumer devices like smart home appliances and vehicles loaded with small computers to provide intelligent functionality. These intelligent appliances connect to the Internet for remote control and administration. Having computers on these things, it may not be long until we can see malware on these devices too.

Remember that appliance manufacturers are not IT companies; hence, they may not have the capability to implement data security in their products. A hacker compromising a manufacturer's server could trigger a firmware update on connected appliances and make it perform additional functions, including attacking other servers on the Internet. It may sound like an event from a science-fiction movie, but this reality is possible.

What is the Difference Between a Malware and a Virus?

Many people confuse malware with viruses. A virus is a type of malware, while malware include viruses and other malicious software.

The first malware were viruses, and developers wrote antivirus software to eliminate these malicious programs. Even when viruses evolved to other forms, people still call them viruses and antivirus companies are using the same term even if they are targeting other malware variants.

Viruses are no longer common on their original form. With antivirus vendors constantly updating their algorithms, malware developers have to come up with new variants to avoid detection, often employing social engineering to propagate malware faster by tricking victims to install it along with legitimate software.

If we look at how malware developers remain active over the years, we can surmise that it is a financially rewarding business; therefore, we can expect cybercriminals to continue developing better malware while antivirus companies play catch-up. The only way to combat malware is to understand the threat it presents, how it spreads and propagates, how to detect it, and how to remove.

What are Potentially Unwanted Programs (PUPs)?

People love free software; however, developers need to earn money too. Malware developers see this as an opportunity to spread malware while providing revenue to free-software developers. What they come up with are installers for legitimate software that also install malware during installation. Antivirus companies call these Potentially Unwanted Programs instead of malware since victims give explicit permission to install them. They have no way of knowing if users allow the installation on purpose or unknowingly installs them.

Why would Users Give Permission to Install PUPs?

Most users do not bother reading user agreements that installers display during installation. Instead, they simply click on the default buttons or press enter. Even if users will read the agreements and prompts, some may not understand the message and assume that they are installing software that is necessary for the main program to work. Unfortunately, PUPs are easy to install, but are often frustrating to remove from the system. Most have more than one instance running such that removing a copy will trigger the second copy to re-install it. Many recent PUPs affect users' browsers, which can be very annoying.

How to Detect the Presence of Malware?

Users familiar with their computer will sometimes notice unusual behavior. Some are obvious, like the browser's looks suddenly changing. Other users may lose their files or the file types are changed. Users may even see system errors that were not present before.

Some changes are not visual, like a program accessing the hard disk and making noise even when the computer is idle. Malware accessing an external server can slow down Internet connection. Infected computers can also be unresponsive when hidden processes are running and using up the computer's memory.

Before assuming that malware may be causing the problem, try restarting the computer and leave it for a few minutes without running any program. If the computer is still slow, then there may be an unwanted background program running, but it still needs confirmation.

On Windows, check the hard disk space by opening any folder and clicking Computer on the left. A hard disk with very little space can slow down the computer and malware may not be the cause.

If there is plenty of hard disk space available, run the Task Manager by holding Ctrl+Alt+Del and selecting it from the menu. Click on the Performance tab and observe the real-time graph. Both the CPU and memory usage should be relatively flat if the computer is idle. An active graph could mean that a hidden program is busy. Click the Applications tab to confirm. There should be no application listed if the user did not execute a program. If there is no program listed and the CPU or memory graph is active then there could be a malware running in the background.

To see the process that is using up the memory, click on the Process tab, then click Memory to display the list in descending order. Check its Image name and description. Right-click on a name, then select Properties to get more details. Use a search engine to validate suspicious names.

The Networking tab can also give clues on the presence of malware. There should be no network activity if the computer is idle. If the network is slow and this graph is active, then a hidden program is accessing an external server or computer.

These are just some ways of detecting the possible presence of malware. Without knowing what the malware exactly is; however, it could be difficult to remove it manually.

Most leading antivirus software can detect and remove malware. For home users, there are free versions available that offer basic protection with the option to purchase upgrades for additional features.

A Note on USB flash drives

With the popularity of USB flash drives, spreading malware via USB is easier. Malware can automatically execute when the user opens a USB flash drive. Once in computer memory, inserting another USB drive will infect it. To prevent this, do not view the contents of a USB flash drive after it mounts. Instead, right-click on the drive's name or icon, then select the scan option from the antivirus. This will remove malware in the flash drive before using it.

If there are signs that a USB drive is infected, but the antivirus does not detect it, install another antivirus program. Some antivirus solutions are not good at detecting USB-based malware.

Antivirus solutions can prevent the installation of malware to some extent. However, there are malware that can still get through if the user is not aware of how they propagate. The best way to prevent malware from infecting computers is to understand how each type works.

The succeeding chapters give an insight into the various forms of malware. It also provides information on how they spread so that users can avoid infecting their computers. Prevention is still the best cure against malware. However, avoiding malware is not easy.

Chapter 2 – Virus

Viruses are the earliest forms of malware and they date back to the time before personal computers became popular. A virus is simply a program that can replicate itself on the same computer. Even without malicious intent, creating many copies of a virus code can quickly fill up the memory and slow the computer down. However, an unmodified virus cannot spread to other computers by itself even if the computers are on a network. Getting the virus inside a computer is the challenge for virus creators.

To avoid detection, virus creators modify legitimate programs by inserting malicious codes. When these programs launch, the virus loads into memory and scans the computer for other executable codes to infect. The virus code stays active in memory until the computer shuts down and the cycle starts again if the user runs the infected program.

Boot Sector Virus

Some viruses attack the boot sector of the computer's bootable disks. The boot sector is an area of a disk that a disk drive initially reads and loads into memory. It contains the startup code that will load other components of the operating system. When the boot sector is infected, the virus loads into memory every time the computer starts, ensuring that it is active without waiting for the user to run an infected program. Since the disk operating system can fit in diskettes in the early days of personal computers, starting a clean computer with an infected bootable diskette can also spread the virus to that computer.

Be Careful when Using Shared Resources

Viruses can spread through sharing. When a user mounts a removable storage media on an infected computer while a virus is active, the virus attempts to infect programs that it finds on the mounted media as well. In the early days, this applies to floppy diskettes and external hard drives, but infections are more common today on flash USB drives.

Once the user connects an infected storage to another computer and runs an infected program, the virus activates and infects the other programs in the new computer as well. This makes users who mount USB drives on shared computers at risk if the computer has no sufficient antivirus protection installed. For this reason, avoid connecting USB drives at Internet cafes and on other public computers.

Even shared documents can carry viruses. Some productivity software allows scripts or macros to automate common tasks. Scripts and macros are small, but powerful programs; hence, they can spread viruses, too. Executing an infected macro will also compromise other documents on the same computer. Worse, sending a copy of an infected document can also infect the receiver's computer.

Are Early Viruses Malicious?

Some early viruses started as programming challenges. There was a game that was named Core Wars where the objective is to create a program that loads in memory, then replicate and terminate other programs running on the same memory space. The competing programs create copies of the code while overwriting enemy codes to terminate them. The program that remains in control is the winner.

Other early versions are simply annoying. Two programmers wrote the Brain virus because users were illegally copying their diskettes. The Brain virus simply displays information about the programmers. The Brain virus spread to computers in other countries.

Computers were not widely connected before and the worst thing that a virus can do is to delete files or make them inaccessible. This is exactly what early destructive viruses did. Some programmers wrote viruses that display something interesting while deleting computer files.

Birth of Antivirus Companies

It was not long before other programmers started writing codes to remove viruses, turning the process into a never-ending game of cat and mouse. Virus creators are continually discovering new computer vulnerabilities that they can take advantage of, while antivirus developers update their codes to combat new virus strains. It has become a never ending battle between malware developers and antivirus companies.

Antivirus programs initially identify specific viruses using their signatures. Signatures are like patterns or fingerprints that identify specific viruses. Virus creators responded by continually creating virus variants that require new methods of detection to keep up. This is why antivirus programs update their databases almost daily.

Antivirus can only play catch up if they rely solely on signatures. Modern antivirus programs detect possible viruses by their behavior in addition to signatures.

Most free antivirus software in the market can eliminate common virus threats so not having one installed is not an excuse. While they retain the name, current antivirus software can detect and remove other forms of malware. To enable additional protection, users can purchase additional features.

However, those who do not have a budget for paid features can still protect themselves from malware. The key is to understand how other forms of malware spread. The next chapters will explain these.

Chapter 3 - Worms

While viruses were a threat due to their ability to replicate, it is not a tool for mass infection because it cannot spread to other computers. The capability to spread over the network by itself is a feature of worms. Networks include local area networks (LAN) that are commonly found in offices, Wide Area Network (WAN) for remote offices, as well as worldwide networks like the Internet.

Early worm research had good intentions and started as helpful ideas. One worm crawls networked computers at night to run processor-intensive tasks, but saves the work and stays idle during the day so people can use the computers normally. It is a good idea that maximizes computer resources, similar to how modern cloud computing works. However, a programming error caused the computers to crash and they had to write another program to remove it.

Another programmer wrote a seemingly harmless worm to check the size of the Internet. The worm creates copies on target computers as it moved from one computer to the next. Due to a programming decision, it can install a copy even if it already exists on the same computer. Multiple running copies of the same worm can slow down the computer until it eventually crashes. A single worm was able to crash a big part the Internet.

Worms spread across the network by exploiting operating system and application vulnerabilities and taking advantage of insufficient data security practices. Nowadays, worms can also spread through social engineering. Social engineering is a technique used by hackers to trick users into unknowingly breaking standard data security precautions. Hackers can bypass a highly secure environment using social engineering.

Operating systems, or OS, are programs that manage computers and network equipment. Just like any program, it can have unintentional bugs and updating usually fixes the problem. Worms take advantage of these vulnerabilities to compromise the system.

If the OS or application developer releases an update before someone announces the vulnerability, then users have time to update the operating system before a malware exploits the vulnerability. This is why users should install updates especially if the patch is to address data security issues. Allowing automatic updates usually takes care of this, although there is a risk of automatically installing buggy updates.

On the other hand, if a malware creator releases a worm before the developer discovers the bug and releases an update, what we have is zero-day vulnerability. Modern antivirus companies address this by developing algorithms that detect malicious behavior. However, very aggressive antivirus solutions may lead to false positives.

False positives result when a scan reports the presence of malicious code when there is none. A good antivirus has few false positives. Third party evaluations can determine effective antivirus solutions with fewer false positives.

Mass-mailer worms

Worms can access email clients on user computers and use it to email copies of the worm to contacts in the address book. Some of these emails can trick recipients into downloading and installing the attachment, compromising the receiver's computer in the process. When this happens, that computer also becomes a mass-mailing tool. Unfortunately, these worms can also get a name from the address book and change the From field with this name. This means that the sender in the email may not be the email source, making the source difficult to track.

Aside from possibly compromising recipients' computers, mass mailers can also slow down network performance. If a worm infects several computers on the same network, then it could eat up all the allocated bandwidth. Worse, data security companies may include the computer's IP address in the blacklist for spamming. This can affect all computers in the network that shares the same public IP.

This is because most offices and home networks use a single public IP address for their router while individual computers get private IP addresses. Worse, some DSL subscribers may get a banned public IP address when their router restarts.

Always be wary of unsolicited emails with attachment even if it comes from a trusted source. A possible indicator of spam mail is when the receiver's name is not mentioned in the salutation. Bad grammar is also a sign of possible spam email.

Do not assume that the antivirus can catch all worm variants. Some worms change the file extension of the attached file. Users may think that they are opening an image file when in reality they are executing a worm. Worms do this by adding a .jpg to the filename, like picture.jpg.exe. Since many users configure their computers to hide the file extension, they do not see that the real extension is .exe because the filename they see is picture.jpg.

Some mass-mailer worms simply send spam advertisements. While they may not do damage to a user's computer, they can still trick victims into purchasing illegitimate products. These emails often have a web beacon, a small image that is loaded from an external server. Displaying this image will send the user's email address to the server, thereby validating that it is an active email account. It will then be a target for future spam emails.

Note that spammers do not use their own computers to send mass emails. They use email worms to prevent authorities from easily tracking them.

Worms for Phishing

Mass-mailer worms provide a great platform for quickly distributing malware. Malware creators use these worms to transport different payloads depending on their intention. One application of mass-mailers is for phishing.

Phishing is a form of identity fraud and is usually for stealing personal information for financial gains. It works this way.

Malware creators will copy a legitimate website's looks, specifically the login and profile pages. Websites of financial institutions like banks and payment platforms are examples of these. Next, they will create an email that looks like an official document coming from the target institutions. These emails often have a sense of urgency, requiring the user to log in to the website immediately to validate or change the password for security purposes. It will also include a link to the appropriate page for the user's convenience.

There lies the trick. Instead of linking to the legitimate page, it will redirect the user to the fake login page after clicking the email link. The URL will have the legitimate website's domain name, but with added characters. Some users may mistakenly believe that they are in the genuine site and proceed to log in. After entering the login detail, the next page may even require them to enter their credit card details for validation.

In reality, users can enter anything in the login page and it will be successful. The login page will simply save the credentials entered by the user, then display a page to get other credentials. When in doubt, users can initially enter incorrect login credentials to check if the site can really validate their account. If it accepts a wrong username or password, then there is no validation and the site is a fake.

Another way to verify if a website is a fake is through browsing all the menus and internal links before entering the login details. Malware creators may not go through the trouble of recreating an entire website's content.

To guard against phishing, never click on an email link to log in or change account details. Always type the known URL on the browser address bar. If clicking an email link asks the user to log in, then do not continue. Instead, type the correct URL in the browser's address bar before logging in.

The next chapter discusses other payloads that worms usually bring.

Chapter 4 - Trojan Horse

Trojans are malware that disguise as useful programs or install together with a legitimate application. Its name comes from the Trojan War, a part of Greek mythology where a wooden gift horse had soldiers inside that attacked the enemies while they were asleep to win the war. Similarly, a Trojan pretends to be a useful application, waiting for the user to launch it to execute the malicious code. Once activated, trojans will run in the background to do their designated task.

Trojans do not replicate and spread by themselves. They often combine with worms to infect other computers. Trojans are also common on unsolicited email attachments, while some users download them along with valid applications.

There are several types of trojans according to function.

Root kits

Root kit is not inherently bad. It is originally a tool for system administrators. It becomes bad if the creator installs it on a computer without permission from the owner, especially if the purpose is to do malicious tasks.

Some trojans will modify the computer's system for hackers to gain access. Root kits are tools for administrators that hide in the operating system while providing a back door for their creator. With privileged access, a root kit's owner can do almost anything to the infected computer remotely. Root kits are good at hiding their existence, making them difficult to detect. They can also delete any traces of malware installation. Root kits usually remain hidden until activated.

Bots

Bots are programs that perform automated tasks. Some bots, called spambots, flood websites with spam advertisements to generate traffic for another website. This is common in online forums and is the main reason why websites validate users before accepting their registration details. Some registration forms require the user to type the characters shown on an image to validate that the applicant is human. However, some spammers go around this by hiring humans to solve the test, although it comes at a cost.

A more malicious bot is one that employs brute-force attack on target websites. Most website owners do not build websites from scratch, but simply use an open source Content Management System (CMS) as a starting point. A CMS is a fully functioning website that allows the user to update content without writing a single line of HTML code. There are many templates to choose from, and websites owners can customize further by using their own graphic images. Using CMS, owners can update website content in a few clicks.

Many CMS software have the default username "admin" and some website owners do not bother changing it. Given the default administrator name, hackers only need to guess the password to take over the website and install malicious software. If it is a popular forum, then there is a risk that hackers can steal the member database.

To attack a website, hackers write bots that log into the target website and try to log in with passwords taken from a table of common passwords as well as words from the dictionary. A website that does not limit failed logins in a given period is a good target. Using a network of zombie computers, hackers are able to brute-force attack a website using bots with minimal risk of authorities tracking the attack's mastermind.

Stolen password databases from forums are not safe, either. Using rainbow tables, hackers can use brute-force to find the matching password for a member account. Since many users employ the same username and password on all sites they register to, this allows the hackers to hack into members' accounts on other sites as well.

Remote-controlled Bots

Malware developers can turn an infected computer into a remote-controlled bot that will perform malicious tasks, including attacking another computer. This is how they get away with Distributed Denial of Service attacks. Attackers do not use their own computers to flood a server, but instead, they use a large network of zombie computers from unsuspecting users. This also saves the attacker from bandwidth costs since the computer owner is paying for it. It also makes it difficult to track the attacker after it spreads from one computer to another.

One analysis of an affected computer shows that bots log into a chat server, waiting for commands from its master. Think of an army of sleeper bots just waiting patiently for a command to attack. Developers will typically just let an installed Trojan do nothing until they have an army of remote-controlled bots to launch a large-scale cyber-attack. The attacker then issues the command to attack from the chat server where the bots log in each time the infected computer is running.

Without good anti-malware software, the presence of a remote-controlled bot in a computer is difficult to detect since it sleeps until a command is given.

Keylogger

Some trojans can capture keystrokes as well as mouse movements in the background without the user knowing it. Called keyloggers, these programs can serve as surveillance software for a good purpose. Some parents use it to monitor children's online activity.

Trojan keyloggers can steal passwords and other personal credentials from unsuspecting users. It can wait for specific events, like users opening a login page, before starting to record user actions and keystrokes. It then sends the log to a remote server for its master.

Spyware

Spyware is another Trojan that collects sensitive information similar to a keylogger. However, it is not limited to monitoring key strokes to steal user credentials, but can also gather information about the user's online activity as well.

Adware

Adware is similar to spyware, but simply records and sends users' online activity and behavior as marketing data to marketers so they can display an appropriate advertisement. Some versions will redirect browser searches to advertisements while others will replace the default search engine with an advertiser's search engine.

Adware creators write these malware for revenue generation. Adware that alters browser settings is very difficult to remove. Antivirus software can remove adware from the computer, but usually leaves the modified browser settings. Saving browser bookmarks and restoring to factory settings can sometimes fix the problem.

Ransomware

Ransomware does what its name suggests. After installing the malicious code, it will either prevent access to the infected computer or encrypt the contents of its hard disk. Users will see a message demanding payment to disable the malware. The criminals behind typically employ money transfer services that are difficult to track. Add this to the fact that these cybercriminals usually live in other countries, making it difficult to run after them.

To spread ransomware, cybercriminals typically take over a legitimate website, usually without the owner's knowledge, to install the malware. They can also spread ransomware using drive-by downloads on the compromised website.

Drive-by Download

A drive-by download will allow the installation of malware by simply browsing an infected website. The user does not even have to click a download link. The affected website contains codes that check for browser or operating system vulnerabilities that allow for automatic download. The malware will install a program with a task to connect to another server to download the rest of the malware. The victim may not notice the download due to the initial programs' small size.

Some anti-malware software can warn if a website has malware when a user tries to access it.

Suspicious Packers

In order to avoid detection, suspicious packers compress and encrypt malware code. Good anti-malware utilities are aware of this and are able to detect the behavior of suspicious packers and prevent them from executing.

Removing Trojans

Most antivirus companies have software that can automatically remove trojans. While it is possible to remove Trojans manually, this may be a challenge since many have multiple copies running that can reinstall copies if the user deletes one.

When looking for good antivirus software, try the demo versions first. If satisfied, users can pay for other features that provide complete protection to the computer. Some of these protections include email and web surfing security.

In some cases, antivirus software can remove malware from the system, but not from the browser. If removing browser add-ons and restoring to factory setting does not work, uninstall the browser and download again.

Avoiding Installer Trojans

Among the popular sources of Trojans are free software installers. Software development costs money, and offering it free is not good for business. However, many people would prefer free over paid versions, especially when performing simple or one-time tasks. To address this, developers break down their programs by specific features, then allow third party marketers to offer them as free downloads in return for revenue to the developer. For example, one utility can convert AVI formats to MP4, while another can convert MP4 to MPG.

How can marketers earn money from offering free downloads? They get revenue by offering their services to advertisers. These marketers create installers for legitimate software, then include the option to install software from other companies. There is nothing wrong with that right, except that many users do not bother reading what they are installing. Unfortunately, many of these optional programs are adware that antivirus software tag as Potential Unwanted Programs (PUP).

An installer for free software will first confirm that users want to install the desired legitimate program. After the user clicks on the Continue or Next button, the installer will get the user's consent to install additional software along with a few descriptions of its benefits. Sometimes, the installer will display an End User License Agreement (EULA), something that no one ever reads, but simply agrees to. It is common to see more than one program added in the installation. The problem, however, is that the default buttons will install these extra programs if the user is not careful.

How can users avoid these additional installations, especially if the user is unsure if the other software is required? Most installers have a Decline button for optional installations. When an installer shows the Decline button, then that additional software is probably a PUP. Pay attention to the presence of Decline buttons.

Some installers have no separate dialog boxes for additional software installation. Instead, easy and custom install options are available, with the easy install as the default. What the user may not see is that the easy install option will sometimes install additional software. Click the custom install option when it is available and deselect unfamiliar applications.

Some antivirus may give an alert that the installer has a Trojan. Always scan the installer after downloading. Users can do this by selecting the installer, right clicking then selecting the Scan option to run the antivirus. This is also a good practice after inserting USB devices.

Users can perform additional verification after each installation. In Windows, simply select Programs and Features from the control panel, then click the Installed On tab. Sort the list in descending order. The programs with the current date are the ones included in the installation. Select suspicious programs and click uninstall. To verify applications, enter the program name in a search engine to see what it does.

Chapter 5 – Threats on Mobile Devices

Mobile technology is now a part of people's everyday lives. Smartphones today are very powerful. They are no longer just for voice and text, but for accessing the Internet and playing games as well. Though not as efficient as personal computers, users can perform most tasks on their smartphones.

For those who require laptop capability at more portable form factor, tablets are a blessing. Those who want the small size of a phone, but with a bigger screen like a tablet, can choose a phablet. Mobile computing is now a reality.

As computers, these mobile devices can be targets of malware. To minimize these, Android and IOS, the leading mobile platforms, have screening policies in place to reduce the chances of malware getting into the official stores. Additionally, updates to the operating system often include security fixes for known vulnerabilities to strengthen the security of devices. Installing the latest updates, when available to the user's mobile device, addresses possible malware problems.

By default, users can only download apps from the official stores. This is Google Play for Android and App Store for IOS. However, a checkbox on Android's setting will allow the user to download from any external server. There lies the problem.

The price for mobile apps is quite low compared to their PC counterparts. However, many users still do not wish to pay for the apps they download, despite their low prices. Malware creators take advantage of this by making commercial apps available for free download on third party servers. By simply deselecting a default Android setting, users can now download a paid app for free.

Unfortunately, for them, these modified apps may contain malware written for mobile devices. Once installed on a mobile device and executed, these malware take over the device and do what PC malware often do. Some malware may steal user credentials while others may display unwanted advertisements. These malware can make the devices very slow, rendering them unusable. Restoring to factory settings may be the only option for some.

IOS has no checkbox to allow downloading of apps from unofficial sites, but bugs in the operating systems can allow jailbreaks. Jailbreaks are IOS hacks that allow users to customize their devices. It also allows users to install unofficial apps. Some of these apps may have malware and can compromise the device.

Malware creators are smart and can always find ways around a secure system. One company created a Windows application that allows users to download apps for free then transfer them to their IOS device. This comes with a risk, however, since some of these apps may also have malware.

Malware creators started targeting IOS developers in China. They did this by making local copies of Apple's development platform since downloading from Apple's official servers is quite slow for developers located in China. Unfortunately, the unofficial installer has malware that infects the apps they are developing. Some of these apps made their way into the App Store before they were discovered and removed.

Another malware creator took advantage of enterprise certificates. These certificates are used by companies to install their own apps on IOS devices without approval from Apple. Malware creators are tricking users to install an enterprise certificate so they can install apps with malware on victims' devices. Many users who do not understand the implications are at risk.

Apple quickly released an update to IOS that prevents this malware from installing. Those who are still using an older version of IOS can also avoid this malware by not allowing the installation of certificates unless it is from their company's IT department.

For IOS users, downloading apps only from the App Store can minimize the risk of malware. It does not mean that Android users are safer, though. Malware writers are invading Google Play by creating fake apps that mimic original apps, but with additional malware. Google has to monitor millions of apps and ensuring that apps do not have malware is not easy. There is a way to avoid potential malware, though. If an Android app asks for unnecessary permissions during installation, do not install it.

Fortunately, antivirus companies now have versions for both the IOS and Android platforms. Installing these apps will help users screen potential malware during installation, as well as remove malware that were accidentally installed.

Conclusion

Thank you again for purchasing this book!

I hope this book was able to help you understand malware threats to prevent them from spreading.

The next step is to check your computers for signs of malware and apply the lessons in this book to avoid infections in the future.

Finally, if you enjoyed this book, please take the time to share your thoughts and post a review on Amazon. It'd be greatly appreciated!

Thank you and good luck!

Book 2

Raspberry Pi 2

By Solis Tech

Raspberry Pi 2 Programming Made Easy!

Raspberry Pi 2: Raspberry Pi 2 Programming Made Easy!

Raspberry Pi 2: Raspberry Pi 2 Programming Made Easy!

Table of Contents

Introduction

Greetings. Thank you for purchasing this book Raspberry Pi 2: Raspberry Pi 2 Programming Made Easy. If you're reading this book then most likely you are here to learn about his nifty new little computer called the Raspberry Pi. In this book, we'll teach you everything that you need to know to get up and running with this little, but powerful computer.

We'll teach you about its parts, its specifications, setting up the operating system, its capabilities and limitations, and ultimately how to do basic programming. We'll discuss the best programming language that works best with the Raspberry Pi and create your first program with it. Without further ado, let's start your Raspberry Pi journey.

Chapter 1: Raspberry Pi - The Basics

What is a Raspberry Pi?

So what is it exactly? We'll it's a small credit-card sized single board computer that is intended to help people learn more about programming, how the computer works, etc. The CPU or Central Processing Unit is basically a system-on-a-chip. What that means is it pairs an ARM processor that is used by a lot of embedded systems and cellular phones with a Broadcom GPU (Graphics Processing Unit), which is a fairly powerful graphics processor that's capable of displaying full resolution 1080p HD video.

The amount of RAM (Random Access Memory) that the Raspberry Pi 2 has is 1 Gigabyte. Its previous iteration, the Raspberry Pi 1 Model A+ and Raspberry Pi 1 Model B has 256MB and 512MB RAM respectively. The RAM is shared by both the CPU and the GPU.

The Raspberry Pi 2 starts at $39.00 and that includes just the board. On the board there are 4 USB ports, 40 General Purpose Input/Output (GPIO) pins, a full 1080p HDMI port, a Network/Ethernet port, a 3.5mm audio and composite video jack, a Raspberry Pi (CSI) Camera interface, a Video (DSI) Display interface, a Micro SD card slot, and a VideoCore 3D graphics core. The GPIO is basically for more advanced users who are going to be adding Arduino accessory boards, ribbon cables for communication with other hardware devices, and major electronics projects; robotics, sensors, etc.

Why Is it Cool to Have a Raspberry Pi?

Most people think the Raspberry Pi is cool because it's a fairly complete computer, it runs on very little power, it's small, and it will not burn a hole through your wallet; it's $39.00, which is less than the cost that you would pay for a dinner with a friend or a loved one. The Raspberry Pi also helps people that are new to computer hardware get into it and get their hands dirty without the cost and risk associated with more expensive standard hardware.

Another thing that's cool about it is that the Graphics Processing Unit is pretty powerful. It can play 1080p HD video, which makes it really attractive to a lot of people as a Media Center PC. In fact, most people buy the Raspberry Pi 2 for that specific reason because it is a cheap multimedia PC.

What Can You Do With a Raspberry Pi?

So what can you do with this thing? Well, just like what was previously mentioned, if you're really new to computer hardware, the Pi can help you learn about those individual components of most modern computers. And if you want to learn how to do programming, the Raspbian operating system that comes with the Raspberry Pi 2 comes with a lot of tools for programming to help you get started.

So you might be asking, why wouldn't you start learning how to program with the computer that you already have? Well, you can. And that's perfectly fine. However, you can think of the Raspberry Pi as your little playground and your test computer that you don't have to worry about breaking if you screw something up. Even if you do break it, you'll only be losing $39.00.

But if you don't care about all that and you don't care about programming or about learning the hardware and so forth, the Raspberry Pi 2 also makes a really great little Media PC. You can get a small case for it, hook it up to the network, install another operating system that's based on Linux called OpenELEC, which is basically a back-end for XBMC (Xbox Media Center), plug it into your TV, and you're ready to start streaming video and audio content on your high-definition TV.

Chapter 2: Hardware Accessories

In this chapter, we're going to talk about some of the hardware and accessories that you're going to need to get started with the Raspberry Pi 2. First, let's start out with the bare necessities. The two things that you'll definitely need are power and an SD card.

Power Requirement

Let's take a moment here and talk about power because it's important. The Raspberry Pi is a little picky about its power source. Learning about what you need here for power could save you a lot of headache later down the road. The Raspberry Pi needs 5 volts. That should be anywhere between 4.75 volts minimum and a maximum of 5.25 volts. It should be at least 700 mAh, but the recommended is 1000 mAh.

The reason for the 1000 mAh recommended power is because when you start plugging in a keyboard, mouse, network cable, and other peripherals, these all pull power away from the system. This is also why some Raspberry Pi 2 users say that 1500 mAh to 2000 mAh is even better. Of course, if you're only doing projects close to your desktop computer and you don't really plan to run the Raspberry Pi 24/7, you could just run it off of your desktop system's power with just a USB cable if you want.

SD Card Storage

There is not on-board storage on the Raspberry Pi. So you need an SD card to run the operating system from and also to store any files. Get at least the Class 4 SD storage. It is recommended that you get the Class 6 or Class 10 if you don't mind spending a little bit more.

However, if it's not available, just get the best one that you can. The cost difference honestly isn't that much, and SD cards are getting cheaper all the time. You'll also need a card reader to transfer the operating system image that you're going to download off of Raspberry Pi's website from your desktop computer to the SD card. You can also buy SD cards with the operating system pre-installed from whosoever your Raspberry Pi vendor is if ever you want to skip the operating system installation on the Pi.

If you want to try out multiple operating systems, you can do that with a single card. However, just keep in mind that you'll overwrite any of your settings that you've played around with in the operating system.

Interacting With the Raspberry Pi

You'll need to decide on how you want to interact with your Raspberry Pi. You can either do it headless over a network, with a keyboard, mouse and monitor, or you can do a combination of both. For network access, you're going to need a network cable; either a CAT5e or CAT6 to connect to your router. There's also a USB WiFi option, which allows you to connect to your router wirelessly.

If you're going headless, you don't really need a USB keyboard and mouse. They are both optional. It just depends on what you want to use the Raspberry Pi for. Just like what was previously mentioned, if you don't want to use the desktop interface, you can skip using a mouse and just plug in a keyboard. If you're using it as a media center and navigate XBMC, a wireless Bluetooth keyboard is a fantastic option if you want to sit on your couch and navigate your media center.

If you're only planning to login remotely using SSH, you can skip the keyboard entirely, or if you want you can just borrow a keyboard and mouse from another machine for the initial setup before you actually go headless over the network. Raspberry Pi should automatically get an IP address from your router. After your router gives an IP address to your Pi, you can just log in to your router to see the exact IP address that was assigned. You can then connect via SSH using that IP address.

If you don't want to find out what the exact IP address is via the router and instead want to find it out locally, you can pull up the command terminal in Raspbian OS and execute an “ifconfig” command. You can then unplugged your peripherals and go headless from there.

Displays

Moving on to displays, if your TV or monitor has an HDMI input, that's great because all you'll need to get is a cheap HDMI cable. If your monitor only has DVI-in, you'll need an HDMI to DVI cable or an adapter. Just keep in mind that if you do that, the audio signal that's coming out of the HDMI port will be ignored when you're using a DVI converter.

Depending on your setup, you can use external speakers or a splitter. If you're going to go headless, you can skip purchasing a separate monitor specifically for your Pi and just borrow one for the initial setup if you want to. Otherwise, you can still do most of the setup across the network if you are connected via SSH.

Raspberry Pi Casing

Moving forward, even though it may look cool keeping your bare board out with a bunch of wires just hanging off, it is probably not the safest thing to do for your Raspberry Pi. So it is recommended that you get a case for your Pi. You can get a prefab case for as little as $5.00. It is completely optional but it does help protect the board. A number of people have made some pretty cool custom cases, all of which are available for purchase on-line.

Chapter 3: Installing the Operating System In Your SD Card

In this chapter we're going to be looking at operating system options and how to actually install it in your Raspberry Pi. First off, you're going to need to consider what your goal is for your Raspberry Pi. Is this going to be a learning or tinkering board? Are you going to be programming or do you just want a quick and cheap home theater PC? For a more general purpose operating system or for the tinkerer and programmer, most people recommend going for Raspbian OS.

The latest version of Raspbian at the time of this writing is Raspbian Jessie Kernel Version 4.1, which was released in November 2015. For a home theater PC, most people recommend getting either OpenELEC or RaspBMC. If you're just not sure and you want to try multiple operating system versions, get two or three SD cards and you can just install a different operating system on each of them. You can swap them out depending on what you feel like doing with your Raspberry Pi. Below is the link where you can download the various operating systems for your Pi:

https://www.raspberrypi.org/downloads/

The Operating system installation method that we're about to discuss is mainly for those who have a Mac or a Linux desktop. If you have Windows, the concept is still pretty much the same. You'll just use a different program to get the disk image onto your SD card with Windows.

Step 1

Regardless of which type of PC you're using, you're going to need to download the disk image or images of your preferred operating system for your Raspberry Pi. These are by no means the only options, just the ones that the Raspberry Pi community recommends in order to get you started. The first one, as we've mentioned before, is Raspbian.

There's also another version that came out called Occidentalis, which is actually based on Raspbian but has a more educational slant to it and includes a lot more educational tools. For a home theater PC, you'll want to install either OpenELEC or RaspBMC. Both of these are built around the XBMC (Xbox Media Center).

Step 2

Once you have chosen your operating system, click the download link and choose a location in your computer that you're going to easily remember. Once your download is complete, it would probably be in a .zip file format so you'll need to unzip it and you should now have an image file with an .img file extension. There are a lot of different methods to get this image onto the SD card, but if you're on Linux or Mac, we're just going to use the "dd" command to write the image on the card.

We're going with this method mainly because it's installed in almost every UNIX-based system and it should work pretty much the same on all of them. Before we proceed in talking about DD in Mac or Linux, if you're a Windows PC user, you're going to need to download the win32 disc imager. Once you've installed it, you need to run it and tell it where the operating system image file is located on your hard drive and what drive letter to write the image to for your SD card.

When choosing the actual drive letter that points to your SD card, make sure that the SD card you're using is blank since everything inside it is going to be overwritten. Getting back to Linux and Mac, you want to open up a new shell or a terminal as it's called on the Mac, and then navigate to the folder where you downloaded your disk image. In most cases it would be in /Downloads/Raspberry Pi/Raspbian.

Again, keep in mind that you will be overwriting everything on the SD card that you're going to be using for this installation. So use a fresh card or one you don't mind overwriting. At this point, make sure you do not have your SD card reader plugged in yet. The reason for this is because we need to find out which device our SD card will be using.

In your terminal or shell, type "df" (without the quotes) and then press ENTER. Now you should see a list of devices and the folders where they are mounted. This should be any of your internal hard drives or external hard drives and so forth. Now is the time when you want to plug in your SD card into your reader and then plug the reader into an open USB port.

Just wait a few moments for the card to mount. This can take a few seconds. After a few seconds, use the "df" command again. You should now see something different; an item that's listed as either no-name or volume/untitled. On the side you should see something listed like dev/disk3s1 or on Linux it would be something similar to dev/sdb1 or sdc1 or something like that next to it.

Drive assignments may vary from user to user so just take which device is listed next to that volume carefully. You want to make sure that you're using the SD device and not one of your hard drives. DD is an unforgiving command and it will overwrite without prejudice and without asking you if you're sure about doing so. So just be very careful. We can't stress this enough. You don't want to overwrite your main hard drive.

Once you know the device that you're going to write to, remember or write it down. Like what we mentioned earlier, it should be something like dev/disk3s1 on a Mac or something similar to dev/sdc1 on Linux. We're going to change this a little bit since we actually want to write the disk image to the entire card not just a partition on the card, which is what we have mounted right now.

So what we need to do now is unmount the SD card's partition before we can write to the entire card. We don't want to eject the card, we just want to unmount it. On your Mac you can open up your Disk Utility. It's in the same folder as your terminal. You then have to select the volume under the SD card device and click "unmount." You can also do this from the terminal, but you'll need to be on the superuser account. So to use Disk Utility using a superuser or root account, you can type the command below:

```
$ sudo diskutil unmount/dev/disk3s1
```

On Linux you would do a similar thing. You would type in the command below:

```
$ sudo unmount /dev/sdc1
```

You can type the command above or whatever your device assignment happens to be. One thing to remember is that the sudo command will always ask you for the administrator password in order to be able to execute the command, regardless of whether you're using a Mac or a Linux system. Once the SD card's partition is unmounted, we're going to run DD with 3 arguments; "bs," "if," and "of." Those stand for block size, in file, and out file respectively. You'll run the command exactly as below:

```
$ dd bs=1m if=2015-12-24-jessy-raspbian.img of=/dev/sdc1
```

Looking at the command above, you're going to be putting a value for block size; specifically 1m which stands for 1 megabyte, for "if" you'll be putting the name of the image file, and "of" is the location where you stored the image file. Regarding the location of the image file, we're going to change that a little bit. For example, if your device is listed as /dev/disc3s1, you want to change the "of" argument to /dev/rdisk3s1.

This may be different depending on your system so changing this will make sure that you use the entire SD card and not just the partition. In Linux for example, the "of" value would probably be something like /dev/sdb1 or /dev/sdc1. In this case, the letter after the letters "sd" could be different depending on your system. So in order to write to the whole card, you just need to take away the number "1." You should have something similar to the one below:

```
$ dd bs=1m if=2015-12-24-jessy-raspbian.img of=/dev/sdb
```

So that's pretty much of it. Once you're confident that you have the correct arguments for the DD command, hit ENTER. You're going to wait a few minutes while the SD card is being written on. At this point, you won't see any output while this process is ongoing. It will probably take a few minutes so just be patient.

If you're on Linux and you get an error, you might need to change the "bs" value from 1m to 1M (capital M). For some reason the case of the letter matters to a Linux system. Once this has been completed, you should be back to a command prompt. And assuming everything worked properly, you will now have a bootable operating system on your SD card.

You are now ready to boot your Raspberry Pi for the first time and start configuring your system, which we will cover on the next chapter.

Chapter 4: Booting OpenELEC & Raspbian for the First Time On Your Pi

In the last chapter, we installed the operating system on the SD card. Let's now go ahead and insert the SD card into the slot on the underside of the Raspberry Pi. Keep in mind that the metal contacts of the SD card should be facing the underside of the board. First, we'll need at least a keyboard, a mouse, and a monitor. Go ahead and plug the keyboard and mouse to any of the available USB ports. Second, go ahead and plug in the Ethernet CAT5 or CAT6 cable on the Ethernet port on the Pi. Make sure that the other end of the Ethernet cable is plugged into your router. Third, go ahead and plug in the HDMI cable for your monitor.

Do not forget to use an HDMI to DVI converter if you have a DVI monitor. Lastly, plug in the microUSB cable of the 5V power supply to the microUSB port on your Raspberry Pi. Once you have everything plugged in, you should see the LEDs on the board start to light up. You will also see that the boot cycle has now started on the monitor. Just wait for login prompt to appear once the boot process has finished.

Logging In

Once you have the login prompt, you want to use the default username which is "pi", and the default password, which is "raspberry" in all lower case. Once you type those in and press ENTER, you're in.

To start the desktop interface just type "start x" and press ENTER. Most people should be pretty familiar with how this desktop works. It's very similar to most other modern GUI interfaces. Let's now take a look at some of the applications that are available to you once you've successfully started the desktop interface of your Raspberry Pi.

- Scratch – This is basically a programming teaching tool. It is very similar to Karel. If you've ever taken a programming class, they use Karel the robot to teach you basic programming concepts.

- Python – Python is basically a very versatile and robust programming language. It is used by many programmers and companies to make web based applications.

- Midori – Midori is a lightweight web browser. It takes its roots from Mozilla Firefox.

- File Manager – The file manager is very similar to the Window file manager. It lets you see the different directories and storage media that's associated with your Raspberry Pi. It also lets you see the important files in your Raspberry Pi.

- Terminal – Since Raspbian is basically a derivative of Debian Linux, it's no surprise that it also has a terminal similar to Linux. It has the same functions as a Linux terminal. It can also run all the terminal commands that you can run in a Linux system.

Now that we've pretty much seen what the Raspbian operating system looks like, let's go on ahead and see what OpenELEC looks like in a Raspberry Pi. Go ahead and mount the image of OpenELEC onto your SD card. The mounting process for OpenELEC is pretty much the same as Raspbian. If you're still logged into Raspbian on your Raspberry Pi, you must log out and shut the Pi down.

You shut the Raspberry Pi down by using the "halt" command. Again, in order for this command to work, you have to be a superuser. So you need to type in the word "sudo," then put a space by pressing the spacebar, type in the word "halt," and then press ENTER.

After you press ENTER, the Raspberry Pi will initiate the shutdown process. Once finished, you can now switch to the SD card with the OpenELEC operating system. Once the card is inserted, you can start booting your Raspberry Pi with the OpenELEC operating system. As you can see, you can pretty quickly change out cards and be up and running with a different operating system pretty quickly.

Once you have OpenELEC up and running, go ahead and explore the different parts of the operating system, see the different programs it has, and find out what it can do. This is the perfect time to explore and learn what the Raspberry Pi and its operating system is all about.

Chapter 5: How to Get Around in the Raspberry Pi's Unix-based Command Line Interface

In this chapter, we will be going through some of the more basic commands that you're going to need to know in the command line shell for getting around the Unix-based file system. If you're running Raspbian, you'll need to know some of the standard Unix commands. Like most systems in Linux or Unix, files are stored in directory hierarchies.

You can also call them folders if you want to feel more comfortable with that term. When you login, unless you have a custom setting, you will most likely begin in your home/username directory. For Raspbian, the default username that we've been logging in with is Pi. So your home directory is going to be /home/Pi.

Most users on the system, except for root, will have their home directory stored within /home. The main exception is the root user's folder, which is stored in /root. On your command prompt you will see your home directory represented as a tilde symbol "~", and you can use that to easily get back to your home folder anytime.

Moving forward, let's get into working with directories. The first thing you might want to know is where you are and what directory you are located in. The first command that we're going to start with is PWD. PWD stands for Print Working Directory, which tells you the current directory that you're located in at that moment. You'll find that most commands in Unix are abbreviations of the activity that they perform.

As you can see from the output after you typed in PWD and pressed ENTER, you're in /home/pi. If you want to change to another directory, you need to use the CD command. For example, if you want to go to the top level directory—also called the root, which is not to be confused with the root user home directory—you type in this command:

```
$ cd /
```

cd / represents the main directory; and the slash that is used is a forward slash. Many people mistakenly use the term backslash when they really mean forward slash. We call the "/" a forward slash because we read from left to right. So a slash leaning to the right is in the forward direction.

Typing the aforementioned command and pressing ENTER will bring you to the top level directory. There is nothing above this top level directory. It only has subdirectories beneath it. With that being said, let's now take a moment to look at a few subdirectories beneath the main root directory.

The first one that we're going to look at is "etc." Etc stores many of the system's configuration files so get familiar with this folder. If you want to change configuration settings, you're going to come here often. To go to the etc subdirectory from the root directory, type in the command below:

```
$ cd /etc
```

Now let's take a look at what's inside etc. We do that using the "ls" command. Ls is short for list and it just lists directory contents. ls also have some options associated with it that allows the user to change the way the listing looks.

Let's go ahead and take a look at a few common options of ls:

- -a – lists all files including hidden files in the directory. Files beginning with a dot "." are considered hidden. So anything that you name with a dot preceding the file name will be hidden automatically, unless you use the -a option to list the files.
- -l – lists all the files lengthwise down the screen.
- -p – puts a forward slash after the directory, which is inside the current directory that you are viewing. This lets you easily distinguish directories from files.
- --color – this will give you a colorful directory listing. However, this

doesn't always work. This command works depending on the system and if you're logging in remotely.

You can also combine multiple options with a single dash. Look at the example below:

$ ls -lap

Typing the command above will give you all the options that you've indicated together with the list command. Now, to go back a directory, you have two options. In this particular case we can either type cd / to take us back to the main root directory since that's where we started before going into etc, or we can type the command below:

$ cd ..

That's "cd" followed by a space, and then two dots. This takes us back one directory. We also have another command below:

$ cd ../..

This command takes us back two directories if you happen to be two subdirectories in. So if you're still in the "etc" directory, go back one directory. There are a number of other directories to familiarize with within the root directory. Below are some of those directories:

- /bin – this directory is for commands and binaries.
- /sbin – this is for system and administrator commands.
- /user – this is for user-related files. It also has its own /bin and /sbin subdirectories.

- /var – var stands for variable. The /var/log subdirectory is a common destination for users who troubleshoot problems whose log file end up here.

- /home – As what we discussed before, this is for the user directories.

- /mnt – mnt, which stands for Mount, is pretty much the mount point for any external drives, image files, or things like that.

- /dev – this is for devices that interface with the hardware.

- /lib – this is for programs and program libraries.

There a lot more, but this is just a quick rundown of the more common directories that you're likely to encounter and use.

So how do we add, remove, or modify files and directories? Well, to create a new directory, type in the command below:

```
$ mkdir directoryname
```

Mkdir stands for make directory. This should be followed by a space and then the name of the directory that you want to create. To remove that empty directory, just used the command below:

```
$ rmdir directoryname
```

Rmdir stands for remove directory. This should be also followed by a space and then the name of the directory that you want to remove. Keep in mind that using this command with a non-empty directory would result to an error. There's another option to remove a directory even though it contains files and subdirectories. However, it can be a little dangerous in the wrong hands if they don't know what they're doing.

So please use with caution whenever you utilize the below command:

```
$ rm -rf directoryname
```

The -r option after the remove command means to do the removing process recursively, which drills down into the subdirectories located within the directory you're trying to remove. The -f option stands for Force, which forces the process to go through. So executing this command basically tells the system that you know what you're doing.

The system will allow you to execute the command as long as you have permission to that file or directory. Again, use these options only if you really need to. There won't be any dialogue box, pop-up window, or anything like that to save you from making a mistake with this command.

For copying files and directories, you'll be using the CP command. Look at the example command below:

```
$ cp filename1 filename2
```

First type in the cp command, followed by a space, followed by the name of the file to copy from, followed by another space, and then lastly the name of the file to copy to. Note that filename 1 and filename 2 should be different. Also, keep in mind that you need to have root (sudo) access in order to successfully execute this file.

To rename or move a file without duplicating it, use the command below:

```
$ mv filename1 filename2
```

The above command will essentially move the contents of filename1 to filename2. You can also specify directories where files are located. For example, let's say you want to copy the contents of /etc/hosts to your home folder. For that you would use the below command:

```
$ cp /etc/hosts /home/pi
```

Type in the cp command, followed by a space, then followed by the file-path of the file that you want to copy, and then another space, and then followed lastly by the file-path of the location where you want to copy the file to.

To move or copy a directory and its subdirectories, you want to use the -r option, which is again a recursive option.

```
$ cp -r directory1 directory2
```

If you want to find out about any of these commands, you can use the MAN command. MAN stands for manual. If you want to find out more about the cp command for example, you just have to type the command below:

```
$ man cp
```

This will pull up all the information about the cp command and all the options associated with it. The same applies to the mv, rm, and so forth.

Chapter 6: Python Programming in Raspberry Pi

In this chapter, we're going to look at the best programming language for the Raspberry Pi; Python. It is considered by many as a notably powerful and dynamic language that is used to develop numerous application domains. Most programmers compare Python to Perl, Java, Ruby, Tcl, or Scheme. This is why Python is the primary language the Raspberry Pi is designed to operate on.

Below are some of the key features of the Python programming language:

- Superb for programming veterans and also remain simple enough for beginners to understand.
- Excellent scalability. Python is excellent in small projects; even better for large scale ones.
- Extremely portable and is compatible across all platforms
- Hardware embeddable
- Elegant and simple to understand syntax and semantics
- Excellent stability
- Has a huge standard library of pre-built subroutines, codes, etc.

Moving forward, we'll discuss how to get a very simple python program working. In addition, we'll also discuss how to use the Graphical User Interface to code basic python programs. However, what this chapter won't tackle is the nitty-gritty of learning how to program in Python. Python object-oriented programming is a whole topic in itself and is therefore out of the scope of this book.

Python programming in the Raspberry Pi is similar to Python programming using a normal desktop or laptop computer. It's just that with the Raspberry Pi, you're programming in a very portable, cheap, but robust platform. To start programming with Python on your Raspberry Pi, you must first make sure that you've successfully installed the Raspbian operating system.

Using the desktop of your Raspbian OS, click on the Menu option on the taskbar. Clicking on menu allows you to see the sub-menus for Raspbian. Click on the "Programming" sub-menu. Once you do that, you'll be presented with different programming applications for Raspbian. One of those applications would be your Python Editor.

Python Editors vary depending on the version of Raspbian running in your Raspberry Pi. However, the most common Python IDE would be Stan's Python Editor or SPE. Click on that and you'll be presented with GUI (Graphical User Interface) for your Python IDE (Integrated Development Environment).

The main window of your Python IDE is where you'll type the source code of the program that you're developing. To start making our simple Python program, first create a folder on your Raspbian desktop where we will put our python script. Just right click on any empty space on your desktop and click "Create New Folder." Don't forget to give your new folder a name.

Now, let's go ahead and develop a simple "Hello World" program using Python. To do so, go to the code editor window of your Python IDE and type in the following code:

```
print "Hello World"
```

After typing this code in your editor, save it by clicking on the "File" menu at the menu of your Python IDE and then click on "Save." You will have to give your python script a name. In this case, just type in the filename as HelloWorld.py and save it inside the new folder that you have created on your desktop. Take note that filenames should not contain any spaces and that it should have a .py extension. This is the file extension for all Python scripts.

After saving the file, run the program by clicking on the "run" button on the menu bar of your Python IDE. At this point, two things should happen depending on which Python IDE you're using. Some IDEs will pull up the terminal and display the output of the program from there, while other IDEs will have a status bar at the bottom where it will show you the output of the Python program that you just ran.

Regardless of whatever mode of output your IDE uses, it should display the words "Hello World." If you want to run your Python script from the terminal itself and not from the IDE, all you need to do is navigate to where your Python script is located first and run the script from there. To do this, type the command below:

```
$ cd /home/pi/Desktop/foldername
```

The "foldername" is the name of the folder that you have created on the desktop. Once you're there type the below command to display the contents of that folder:

```
$ ls -l
```

Now, you'll see your HelloWorld.py file. To run this just type in the below command:

```
$ python HelloWorld.py
```

The command above is basically telling the system to use the Python interpreter to open the HelloWorld.py file. Press ENTER and you'll see the output; "Hello World."

Congratulations, you've just made your first Python program in your Raspberry Pi.

Conclusion

Thank you for purchasing and reading this book. We hope that we've taught you all the basic things that you need to know about your Raspberry Pi; how to set it up, how to install the operating system so that you'll be able to develop programs using it.

From here, developing more intricate programs using Python is just a matter of learning the nitty-gritty of the programming language itself. There are many online tutorials out there that you can go and see to get in-depth knowledge of Python programming. Python is a very versatile and stable programming language and using it to make your Pi do wondrous things is easy, as long as you have an advanced knowledge of the programming language itself.

Again, Thank you so much and we hope that you succeed in your quest for knowledge on the Python programming language and that you have fun in finding ingenious ways to use your Raspberry Pi.